What's the difference?
Insects

Stephen Savage

RSVP
RAINTREE
STECK-VAUGHN
P U B L I S H E R S
A Steck-Vaughn Company

Austin, Texas
www.steck-vaughn.com

What's the Difference?

Amphibians Insects
Birds Mammals
Fish Reptiles

Cover: A swallowtail butterfly and a seven-spot ladybug

Title page: Dragonfly larva in its final stage; a green tiger beetle

Contents page: The caterpillar of a swallowtail butterfly

Published by Raintree Steck-Vaughn Publishers, an imprint of Steck-Vaughn Company

Printed in Italy. Bound in the United States.
1 2 3 4 5 6 7 8 9 0 04 03 02 01 00

Library of Congress Cataloging-in-Publication Data
Savage, Stephen.
Insects / Stephen Savage.
    p.   cm.—(What's the difference)
    Includes bibliographical references and index.
    Summary: Describes the characteristics shared by all insects and highlights how various species are different, discussing habitats, methods of moving around, feeding habits, and life cycles.
    ISBN 0-7398-1355-2 (hard)
    0-7398-1477-X (soft)
    1. Insects—Juvenile literature.
    [1. Insects.]
    I. Title. II. Series.
    QL467.2.S28   2000
    595.7—dc21   99-13022

Contents

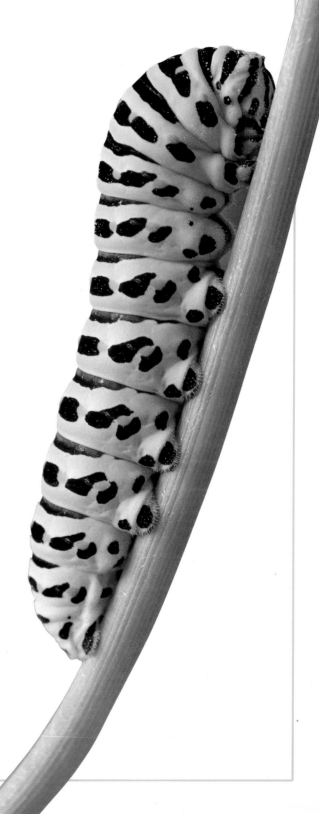

What a Difference!

Insect characteristics

- 🦋 Insects have three parts to their bodies.
- 🦋 Most insects have six legs.
- 🦋 Insects have large compound eyes so that they can see all around.
- 🦋 Most insects have wings.

There are more insects in the world than any other animal. They all have similar features, but their size, color, and shape can be very different.

▼ The largest beetles are male Hercules beetles. With their giant horns, each of these two fighters measures almost 6 in. (15 cm) long.

The young of most insects do not look like their parents. They do not have wings and may have extra legs.

▲ There are many beautiful butterflies and moths. This emperor moth, resting on a tree trunk, has false eye spots to confuse predators.

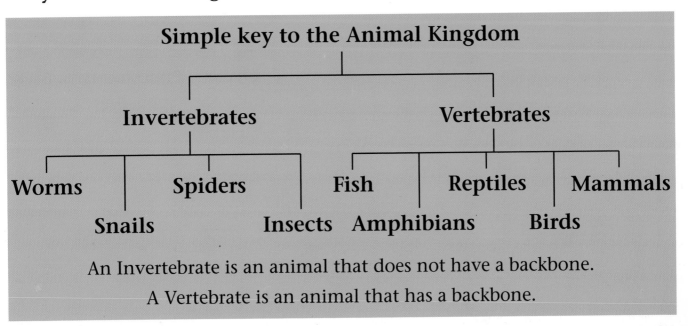

Simple key to the Animal Kingdom

Invertebrates

Vertebrates

Worms

Snails

Spiders

Insects

Fish

Amphibians

Reptiles

Birds

Mammals

An Invertebrate is an animal that does not have a backbone.

A Vertebrate is an animal that has a backbone.

Where Insects Live

Insects are found in many of the world's habitats. They live in forests, grasslands, mountains, deserts, lakes, rivers, and ponds. They even live in towns and cities.

Insects have special features that help them cope with the problems of living in these very different places.

▲ Although the darkling beetle lives in the waterless desert, it obtains water from droplets that form on its body and run down to its mouth.

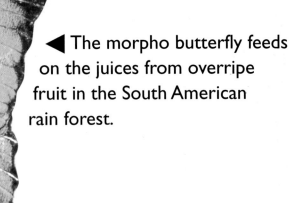

◄ The morpho butterfly feeds on the juices from overripe fruit in the South American rain forest.

Different habitats

- Insects that live in grass are usually green or brown.
- Pond insects can fly from one pond to another.
- Field crickets lay their eggs underground.
- Desert ants collect and store seeds to eat when there is no other food.

The water boatman lives in ponds. It can breathe underwater because it carries an air bubble beneath its body.

Catching a Meal

Some insects eat plants or drink the nectar from flowers. Caterpillars chew the leaves of plants. When they become adult butterflies or moths, most will sip nectar.

Avoiding predators

- Some beetles squirt chemicals at an attacker.
- The caterpillar of a swallowtail butterfly looks like a bird dropping to put off predators.
- Eye spots on a moth or butterfly may frighten off an attacker.

▼ Leaf-cutter ants carry leaves back to the nest. The leaves make a garden that grows a special fungus that the ants will eat.

Many insects are predators. They eat other insects and tiny animals, which they catch with large, powerful jaws. Huge numbers of army ants on the march can overwhelm insects, small mammals, and birds because there are so many of them.

▲ This adult dragonfly waits to catch flying insects with its jaws.

◄ A green tiger beetle feeding on a caterpillar

Insects are eaten by birds and mammals. To protect themselves, many insects have colors that help them blend into their surroundings. Some look exactly like sticks, leaves, or plants.

The two yellow-and-black striped flower ▶ flies feeding in the center of the thistle look like wasps. Most insect-eating animals see the warning colors and keep away.

▼ This praying mantis looks just like a flower. The disguise tricks its prey and protects it from insect-eating mammals and birds.

▲ A katydid in the South American rain forest mimics a dead leaf so that other insect-eating animals will not recognize it and want to eat it.

Many insects, such as wasps, have a sting to protect them or to paralyze other insects. Some may taste horrible. These kinds of insects are brightly colored to warn other animals to stay away.

◄ This close-up picture of a housefly shows its compound eyes, which allow it to see an attacker even from behind.

Hot and Cold

Insects are often active on sunny days but find shelter when it is cold. Many flying insects need to warm their wings before they can fly.

How to keep warm and cold

- Some hibernating insects have a chemical in their blood to prevent it from freezing.
- Mountain insects live at temperatures of around 32° F (0° C).
- Some moths' bodies are covered with hair to keep them warm.
- Compass termites in Australia build a wedge-shaped nest.

◀ This tortoiseshell butterfly is sunbathing. Many butterflies warm their wings in this way.

These North American monarch butterflies, hanging from the branches of a tree, are preparing to migrate to warmer countries to breed. They migrate so their caterpillars will not be killed by winter frosts.

▼ Black ants move their developing young from one chamber to another. This keeps them at the right temperature.

Most ants live in underground nests made up of different chambers and tunnels. Some chambers are warmer than others.

On a hot summer's day, ground-living insects stay in the shade. Many desert insects come out only at night, to avoid the blazing sun.

◀ This beetle lives in the Kalahari Desert in Africa. It has long legs that keep its body off the scorching sand.

Worker honey ▶ bees at the entrance to the hive. They sometimes fan their wings to help keep the hive cool.

Tiny antlike termites build special chimneys on the outsides of their tall nests. The chimneys help keep the nest cool.

▼ Termites in Africa build tall nests to allow air to circulate through the chambers. (Inset) Termites inside the nest

Getting Around

Most insects have wings. Butterflies and other flying insects use their wings to fly from place to place or to escape from danger.

▲ Unlike butterflies that flutter, the flower fly can hover in the air or fly off at high speed.

Some types of insects walk or run, using their six legs. Their wings are covered by a hard wing case, ready to be opened when the wings are needed.

Getting around

- Some grasshoppers can leap 27 in. (70 cm).
- Water beetles can swim underwater.
- Some types of insects have two wings and others have four.
- Monarch butterflies fly thousands of miles when they migrate to breed.

▲ A stick insect walking up the bark of a tree

▼ A green tiger beetle can run 24 in. (60 cm) a second. This speed is equal to a large mammal running 250 mph (400 km/h).

17

A few types of insects can walk on the surface of still water. They eat other insects that fall onto the surface.

The larvae of many insects are able to move around by wriggling or crawling.

Crickets and ▶ grasshoppers can leap huge distances to escape danger.

▼ Water striders have special hairs on their legs that allow them to walk on water.

Caterpillars crawl with the help of many legs. The flying adult will have only six legs.

Insect Young

Insects use various ways to attract a mate. Grasshoppers, crickets, and a few other insects make sounds. Some female insects produce a scent that attracts a male.

▼ Dragonflies lay their eggs in ponds. The larvae live in the water until ready to become adults. This dragonfly larva is in the final stage before it becomes an adult.

All insects lay eggs. Most types of insects lay hundreds of eggs, but only a few will survive to become adults.

▼ The dung beetle lays an egg on a dung ball that it has made from animal dung. The egg is buried with other dung balls, each in a special chamber.

Life cycle

- Insects lay eggs.
- Eggs hatch into larvae.
- Larvae become chrysalises (or pupae).
- Adult insects emerge from pupae.

Some insects take great care of their young. They will even defend them against predators much larger than themselves.

▲ A female shield bug protects her eggs and young with her shieldlike body. The young bugs look just like their parents.

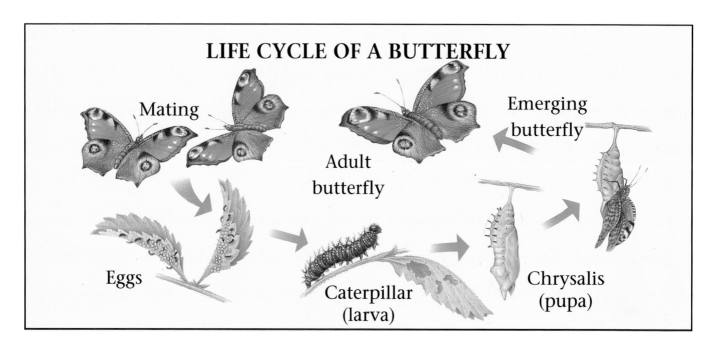

LIFE CYCLE OF A BUTTERFLY

Mating

Adult butterfly

Emerging butterfly

Eggs

Caterpillar (larva)

Chrysalis (pupa)

▼ Honey bee larvae develop within brood cells. They are protected by the rest of the bee colony.

Honey bees and ants live in large colonies ruled by a queen. Most of the colony is made up of workers who collect food and look after the young.

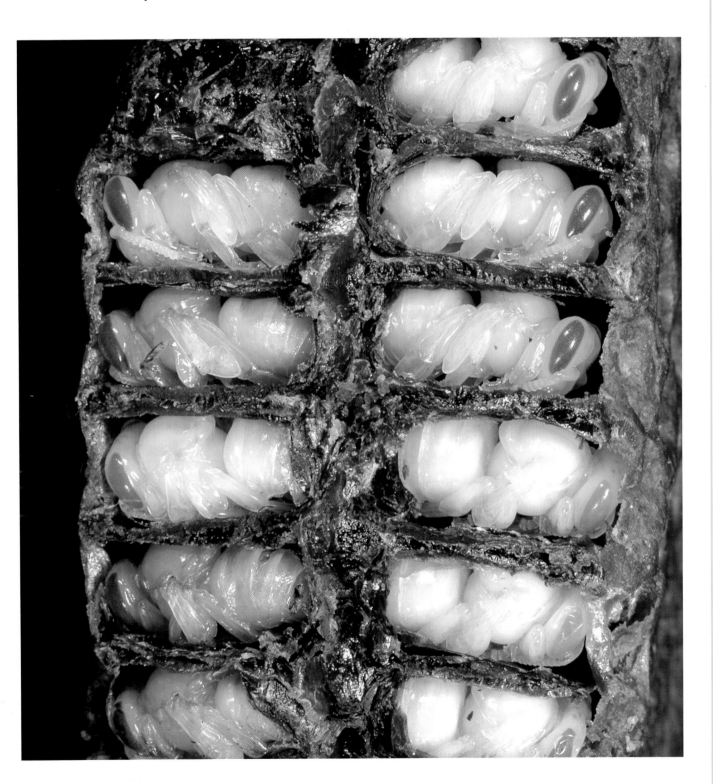

Insect Pets

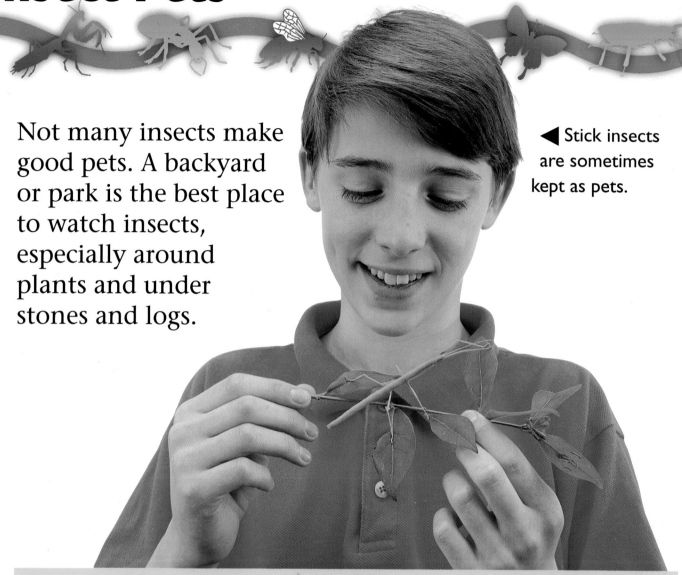

Not many insects make good pets. A backyard or park is the best place to watch insects, especially around plants and under stones and logs.

◀ Stick insects are sometimes kept as pets.

Caring for insects

- You need a tank with a lid and airholes.
- Provide the right food to eat.
- Give the insects twigs and foliage for climbing on.
- If you keep insects in a pond tank, you will need an air pump.

Many insects are attracted to gardens by flowers. They feed on their nectar and pollinate them with pollen from other flowers, so they can reproduce. Insects and flowers need each other to survive.

▲ Keep caterpillars in a tank to watch them change, first into chrysalises and then into butterflies. This red admiral butterfly has emerged from its chrysalis.

Unusual Insects

A few insects are among the most amazing creatures of the animal world. Some are very brightly colored or have bodies that are very strangely shaped.

▲ The back end of the hawk moth caterpillar looks like the head of a snake. This frightens away most attackers.

◄ The bodies of some honeypot worker ants become honey stores, to feed the ant community when food is scarce.

The lives of some insects are so unusual that they appear strange even for insects.

▼ Chemicals inside a female glowworm's body produce a light that attracts male glowworms.

Parasite insects

- Fleas live on the bodies of larger animals.
- A female mosquito bites animals and humans to obtain blood, which helps her eggs develop.
- Aphids suck the juices from plants.

Insects to scale

Adult Human Hand

Swallowtail Butterfly

Morpho Butterfly

Hercules Beetle

Emperor Moth

Dragonfly

Praying Mantis

Adult Human Finger

Darkling Beetle

Water Boatman

Field Cricket

Army Ant

Leaf-cutter Ant

Adult Human Finger

Black Ant, Worker

Honey Bee, Worker

Desert Beetle

Termite, Worker

Water Strider

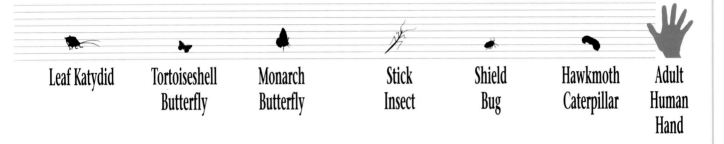

| Leaf Katydid | Tortoiseshell Butterfly | Monarch Butterfly | Stick Insect | Shield Bug | Hawkmoth Caterpillar | Adult Human Hand |

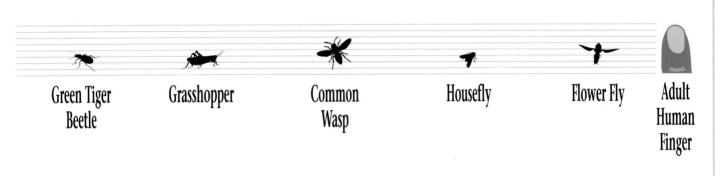

| Green Tiger Beetle | Grasshopper | Common Wasp | Housefly | Flower Fly | Adult Human Finger |

| Swallowtail Caterpillar | Dung Beetle | Honeypot Ant | Glowworm | Mosquito | Aphid | Adult Human Finger |

Glossary

Brood cells The chambers of a bees' nest or hive where the young develop.

Compound eyes The eyes of insects. Compound eyes are made up of hundreds of tiny lenses.

Habitat The natural home of plants and animals.

Hibernate To spend the winter in a state similar to sleep.

Katydid A type of grasshopper, found in the Americas.

Larvae Grubs or insects after they have left eggs but before they become adults. A single grub is a larva. The larvae of butterflies and moths are called caterpillars.

Migrate To move from one region to another in search of food or a warmer climate.

Nectar A sugary substance produced by plants to attract insects.

Pollinate To fertilize plants and flowers with pollen so that they will produce seeds.

Predators Animals that hunt others for food.

Prey Animals that are hunted and killed for food.

Pupa A middle stage between larva and adult insect.

Queen The fertile female among a colony of ants, bees, or other similar insects.

Finding Out More

Books to Read

Allen, Missy. *Dangerous Insects* (Encyclopedia of Danger). Broomall, PA: Chelsea House, 1993.

Burnie, David. *Insects and Spiders* (Nature Company Discovery Library). Alexandria, VA: Time-Life Books, 1997.

Gallimard, Jeunesse. *Butterflies* (First Discovery Books). New York: Scholastic, 1997.

Mound, Laurence. *Insect* (Eyewitness). New York: Knopf Books for Young Readers, 1990.

Pascoe, Elaine. *Butterflies and Moths* (Nature Close-Up). Woodbridge, CT: Blackbirch, 1996.

Ross, Kathy. *Crafts for Kids Who Are Wild About Insects*. Ridgefield, CT: Millbrook Press, 1997.

Videos

Amazing Animals: Creepy Crawly Animals (Dorling Kindersley, 1999)

Amazing Animals: Minibeasts (Dorling Kindersley, 1996)

Eyewitness: Butterfly and Moth (Dorling Kindersley, 1996)

Eyewitness: Insects (Dorling Kindersley, 1996)

Index

Page numbers in **bold** refer to photographs.

Picture Acknowledgments:

Bruce Coleman Ltd 26(lower), /M.P.L. Fogden 4, /Andrew Purcell 5, /David Hughes 6(top), /Luiz Marigo 6(lower), /Kim Taylor 7, 9(top), /Andrew Purcell 9(lower), /Jenny Grayson 10(top), /Kevin Rushby 10(lower), /Luiz Marigo 11(top), /Kim Taylor 11(lower), /Harold Lange 12, /Ingo Arnot 13(top), /Jeremy Grayson 13(lower), /Kim Taylor 14(top), /Janos Jurka 15, /Kim Taylor 15(inset), 16, /Leonard Lee Rue 17(top), /Andrew Purcell 17(lower) and title page, /J. Brackenbury 18(top), /Kim Taylor 18(lower), Jens Rydell 19 and contents page, /Jane Burton 20 and title page, /Kim Taylor 21, /Frieder Sauder 22, /Kim Taylor 23, /Jane Burton 25, /Peter Evans 26(top), /Peter Hinchcliffe 26(lower); Discovery Books 24(lower); FLPA /B. Borrell cover (inset), /Chris Mattison 14(lower); Oxford Scientific Films /David Dennis; Tony Stone Worldwide /A. Bumgarner cover; Wayland Picture Library 24(top). Artwork on pages 28-9 by Mark Whitchurch and on page 22 by John Yates.